Improvisations on a theme by Michelangelo

Motifs From the Sistine Chapel Painting of the Garden Of Eden and the Expulsion

All Artwork Created by Randy Dillon

Improvisations on a theme by Michelangelo

Motifs From the Sistine Chapel Painting OF the Garden and the Expulsion

First Edition

by Randy Dillon

Veroglyphic Publishing
2009

Table of Contents

Michelangelo's painting on the ceiling of the Sistine Chapel is considered by many to the the quintessential artwork not only of Michelangelo's life, but also in the sponsorship of the Roman Catholic Church into the arts. Many refer to the work as Michelangelo's ceiling.

I have decided to take upon as a project to create improvisations of two sections of Michelangelo's Ceiling having to do with the motifs of the Garden of Eden.

In all, there are twelve original works of art with fifteen close-ups to give a better view of how the interpretations played out among the major characters within the theme.

Temptation

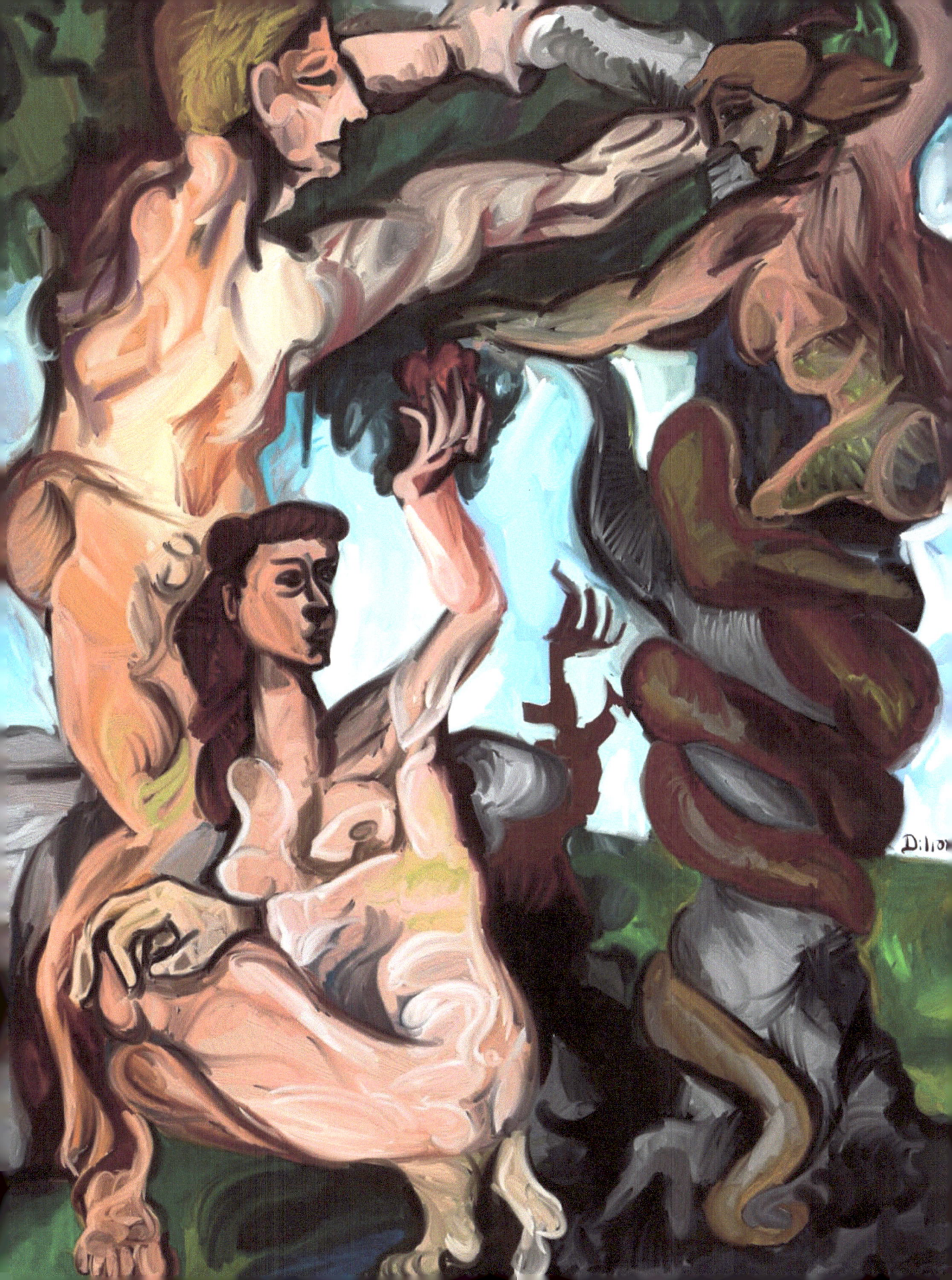

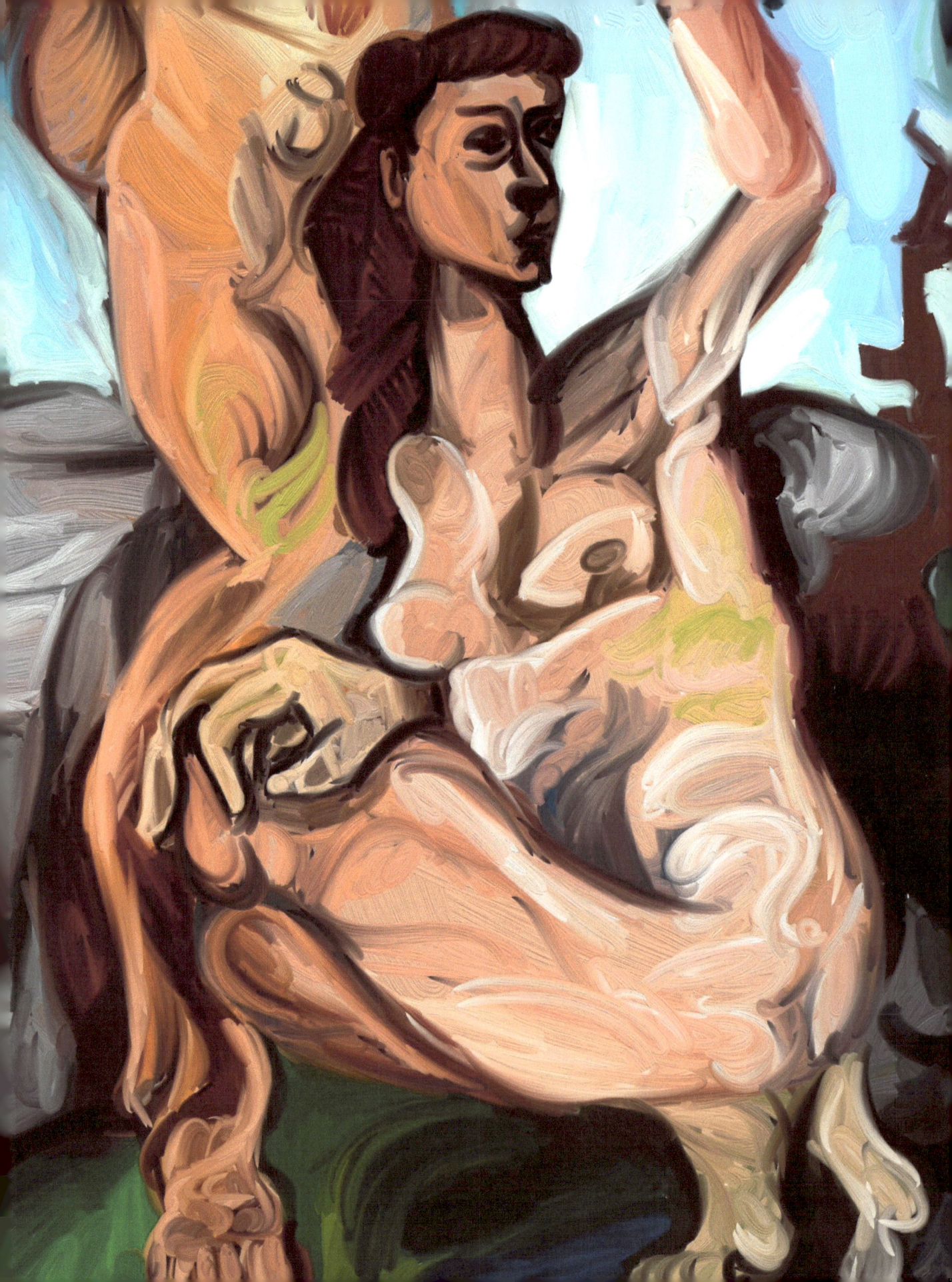

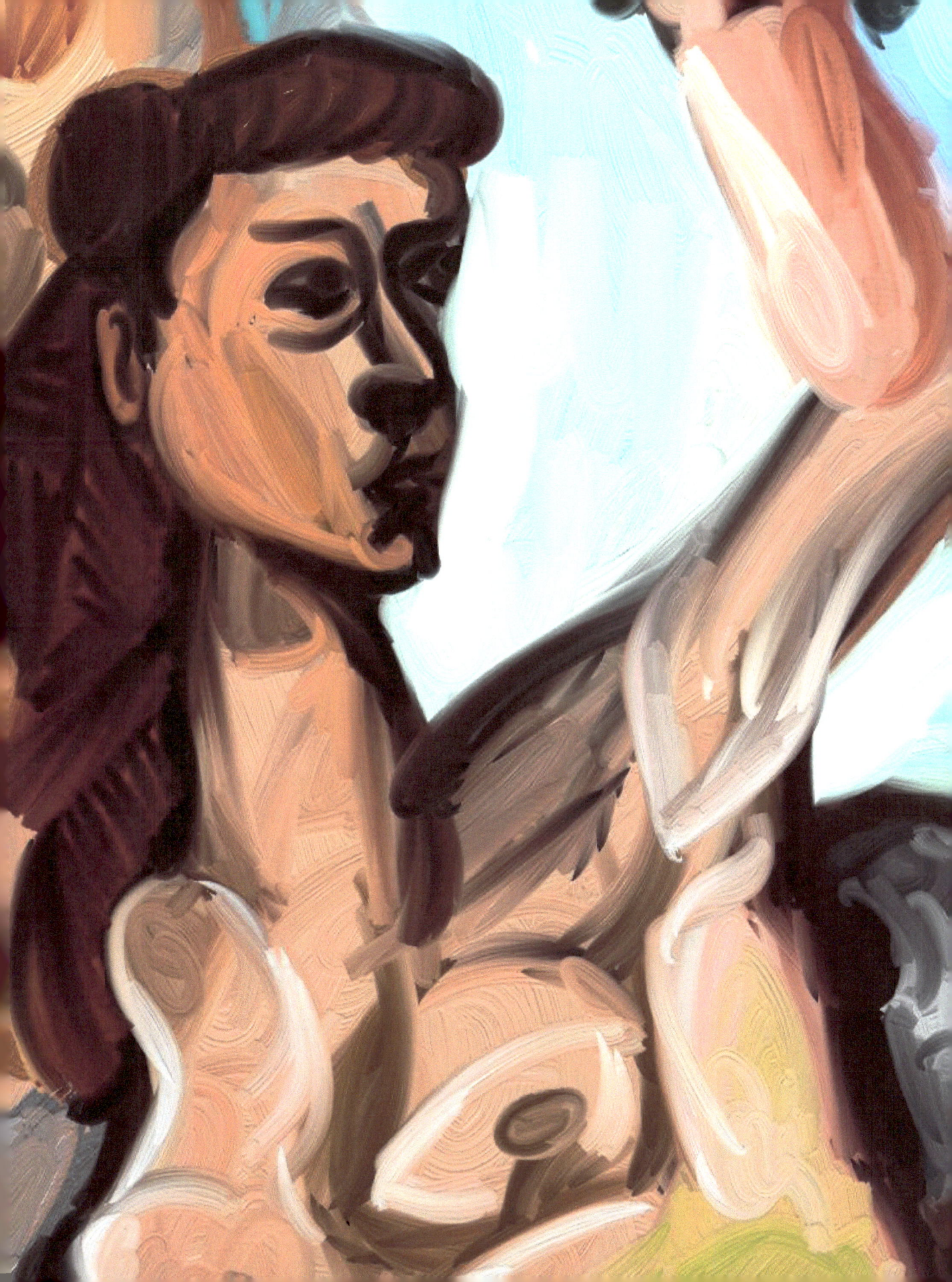

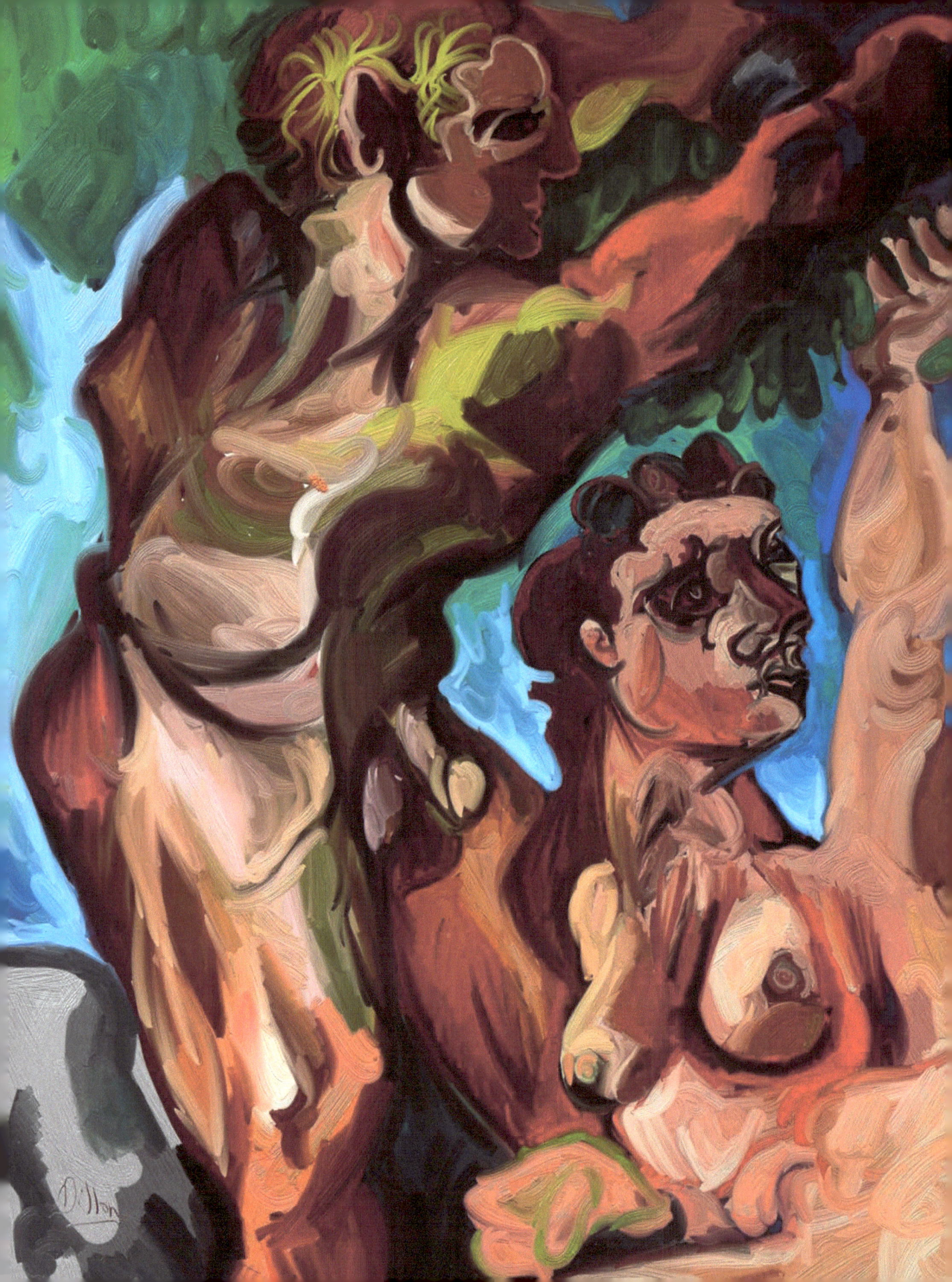

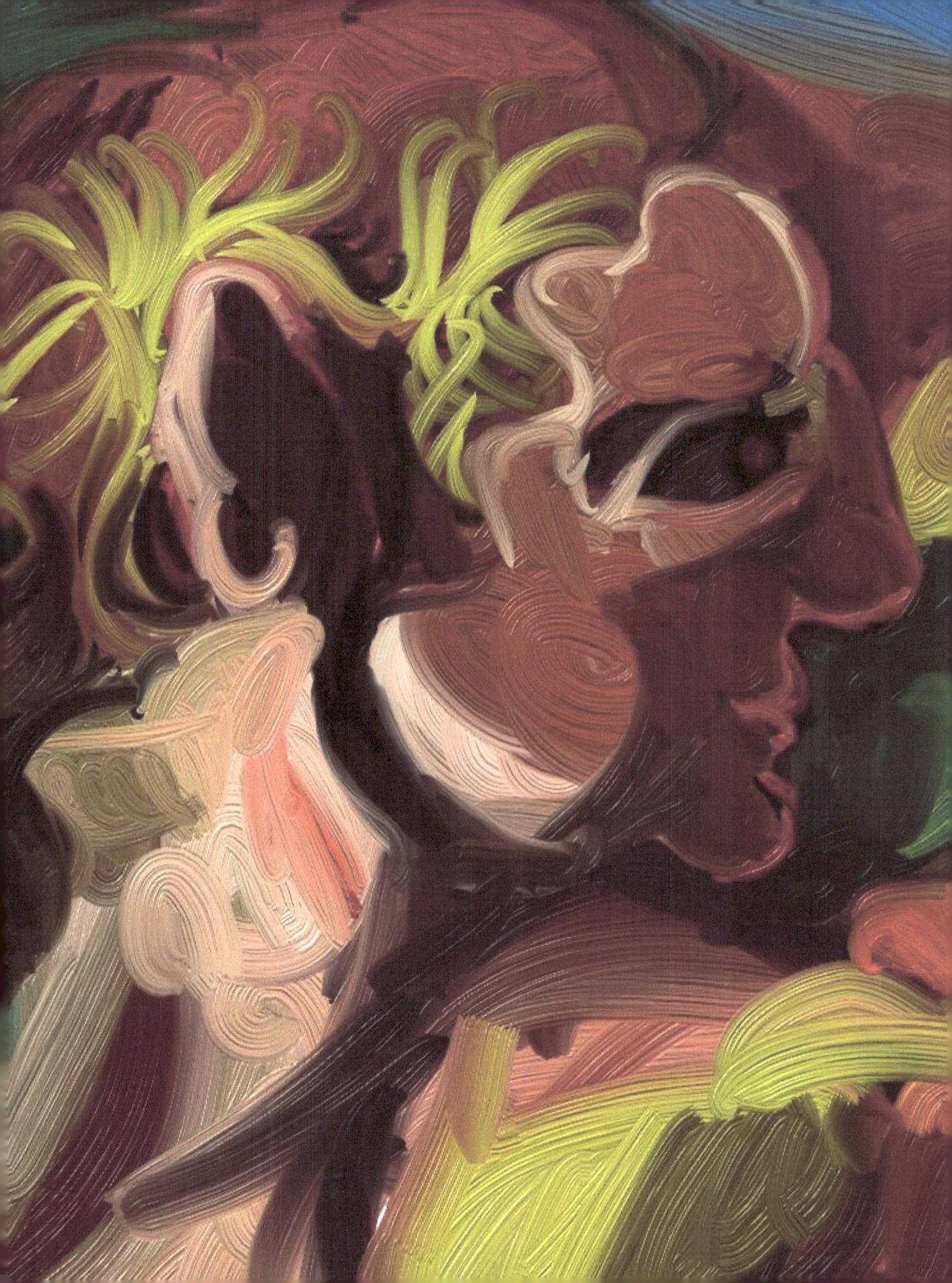

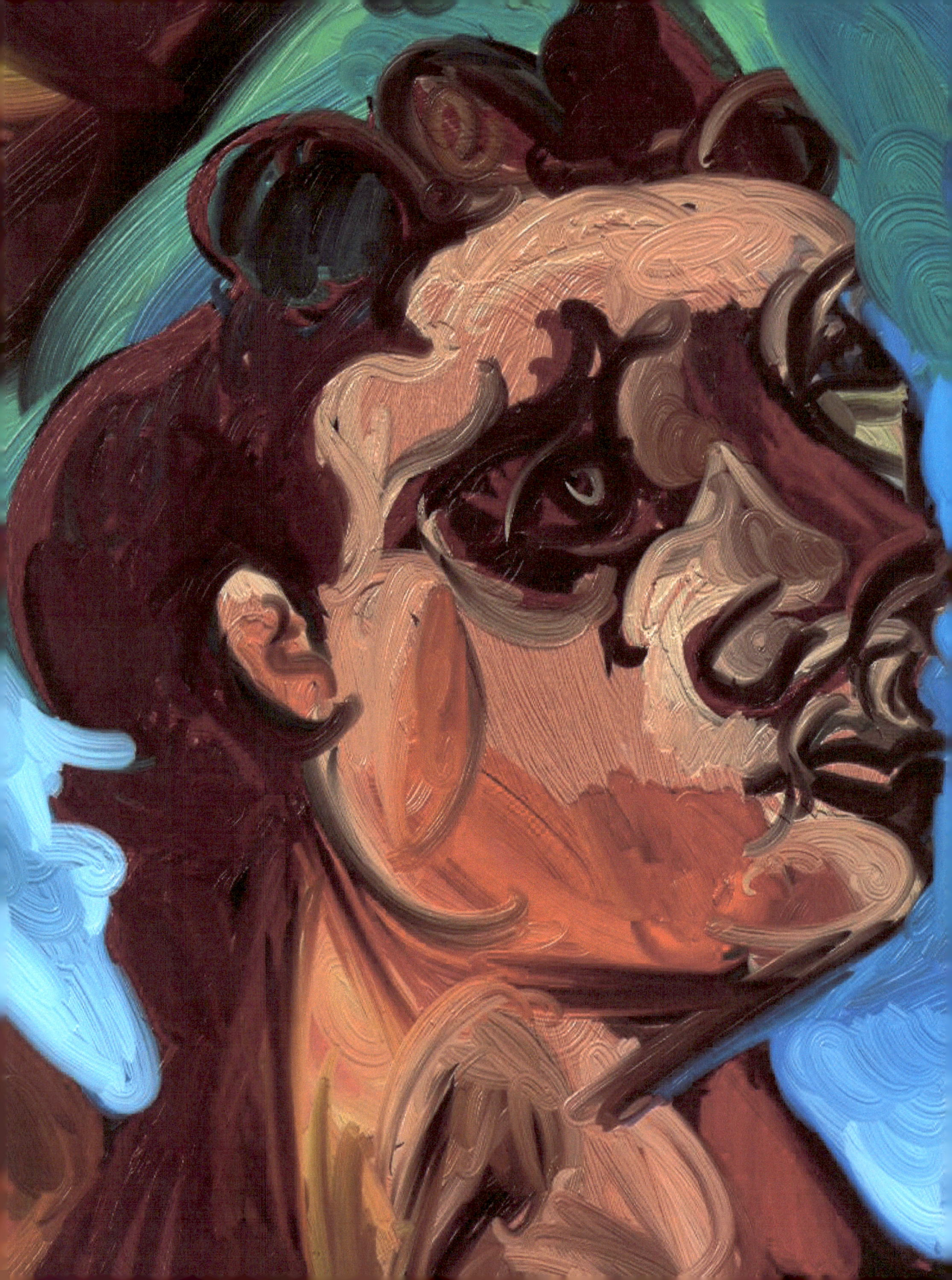

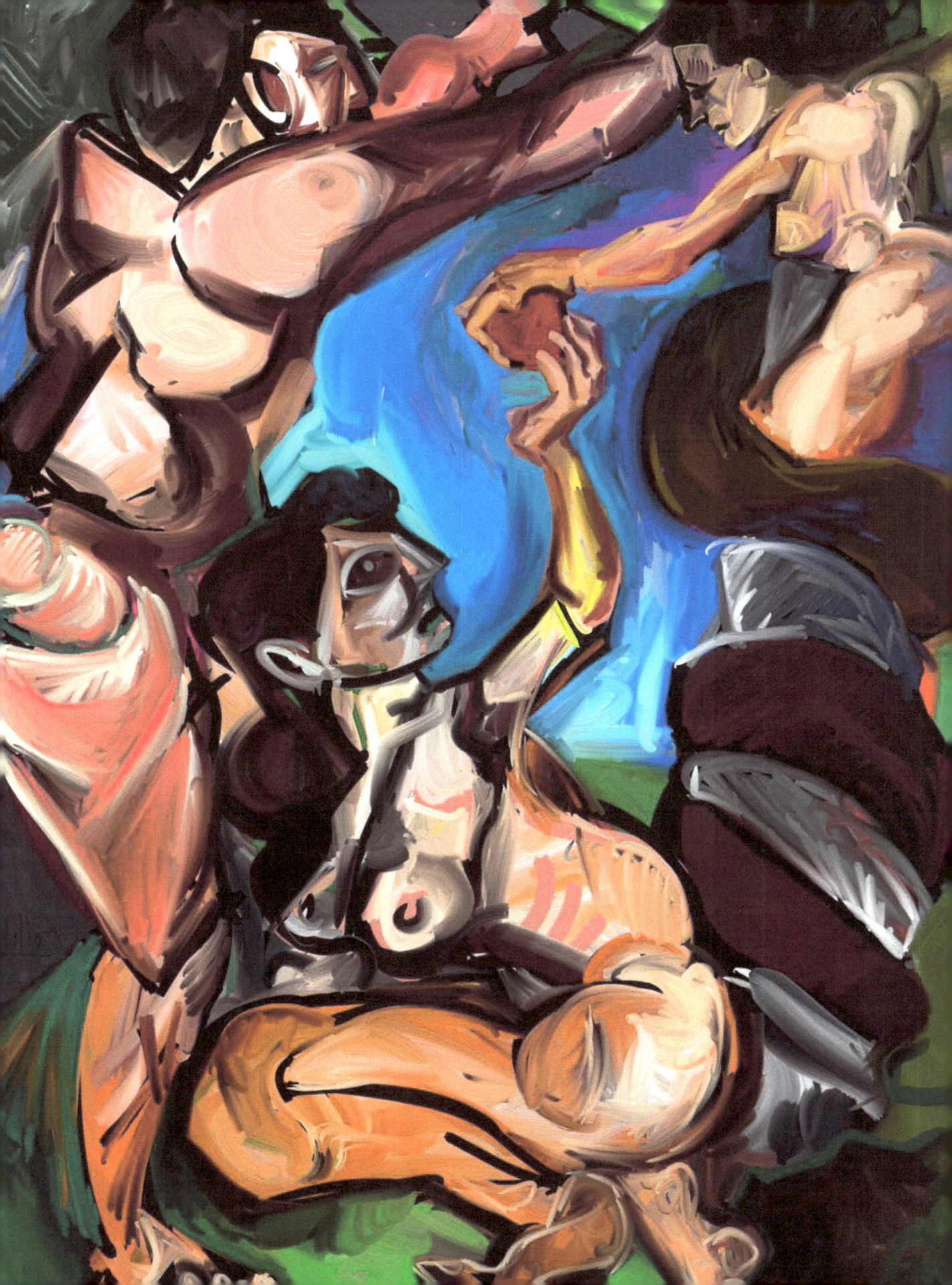

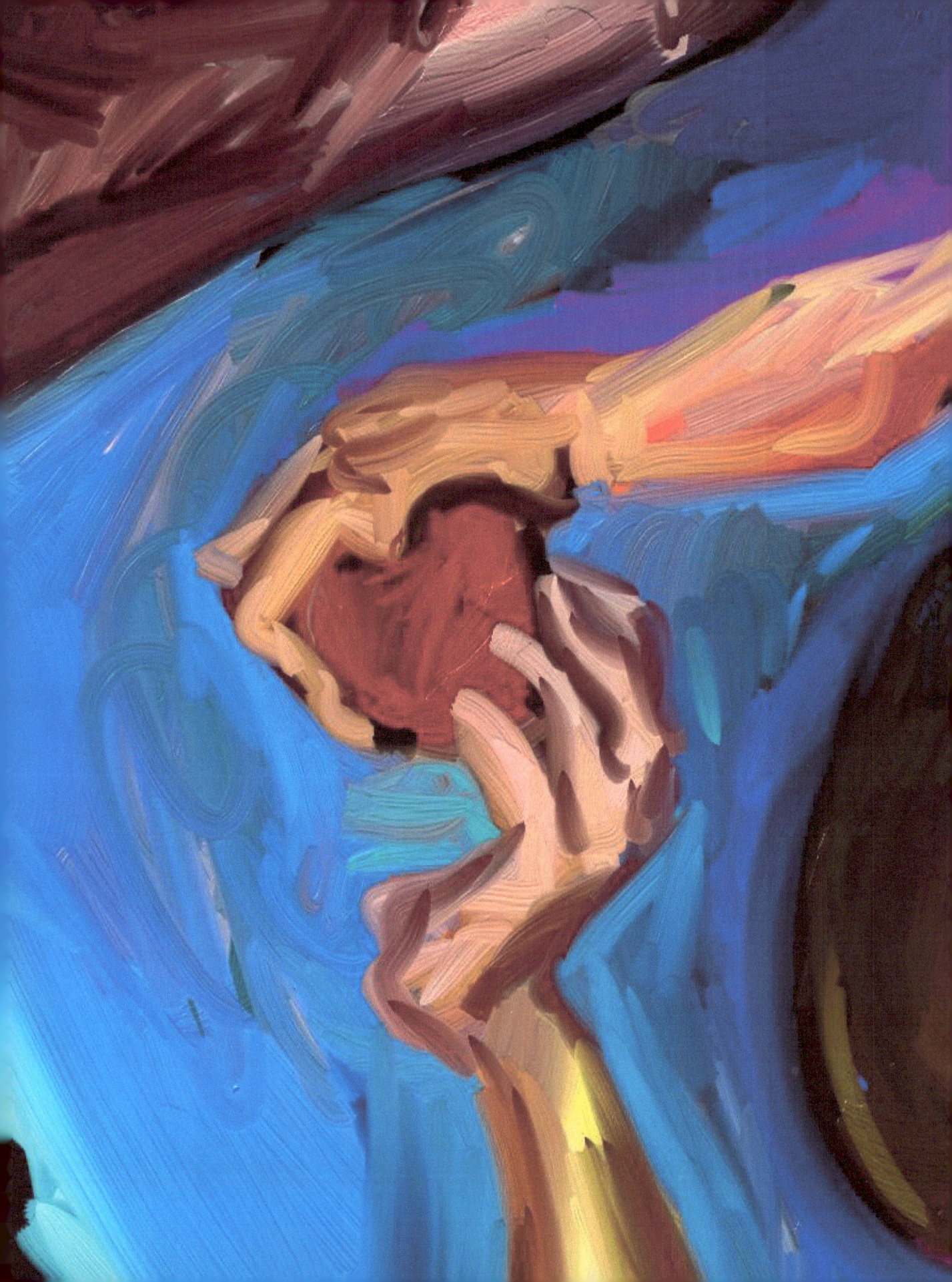

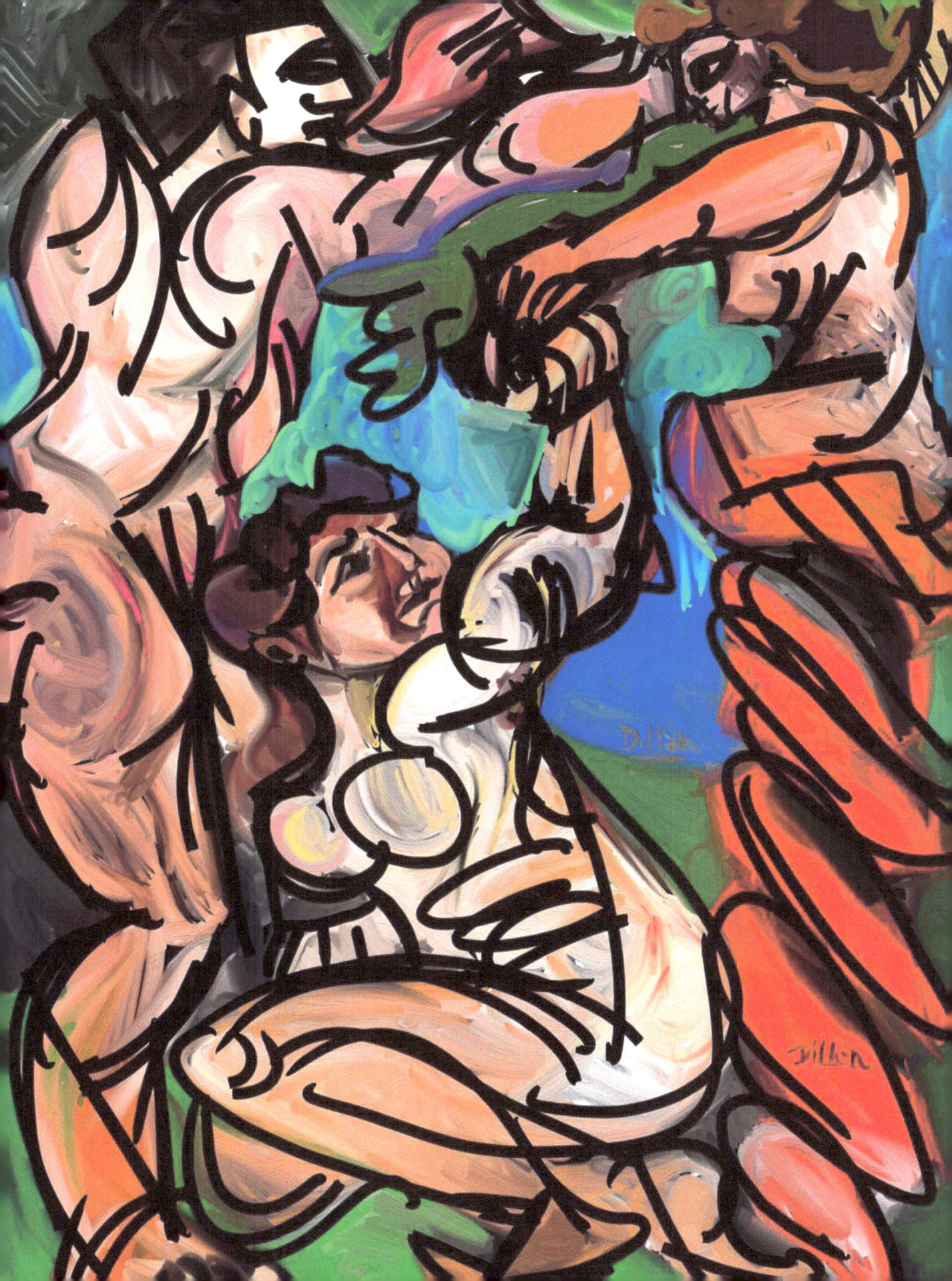

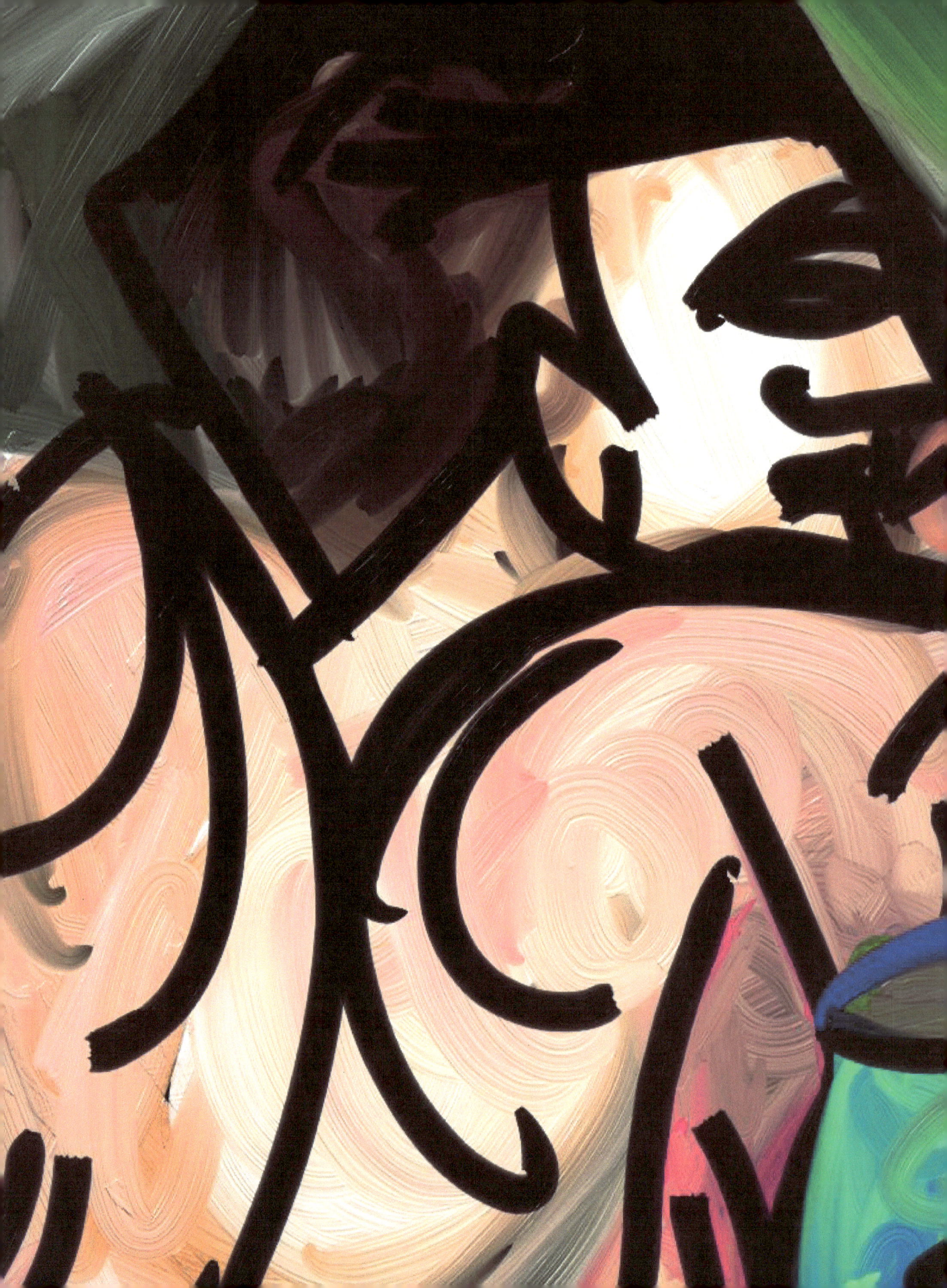

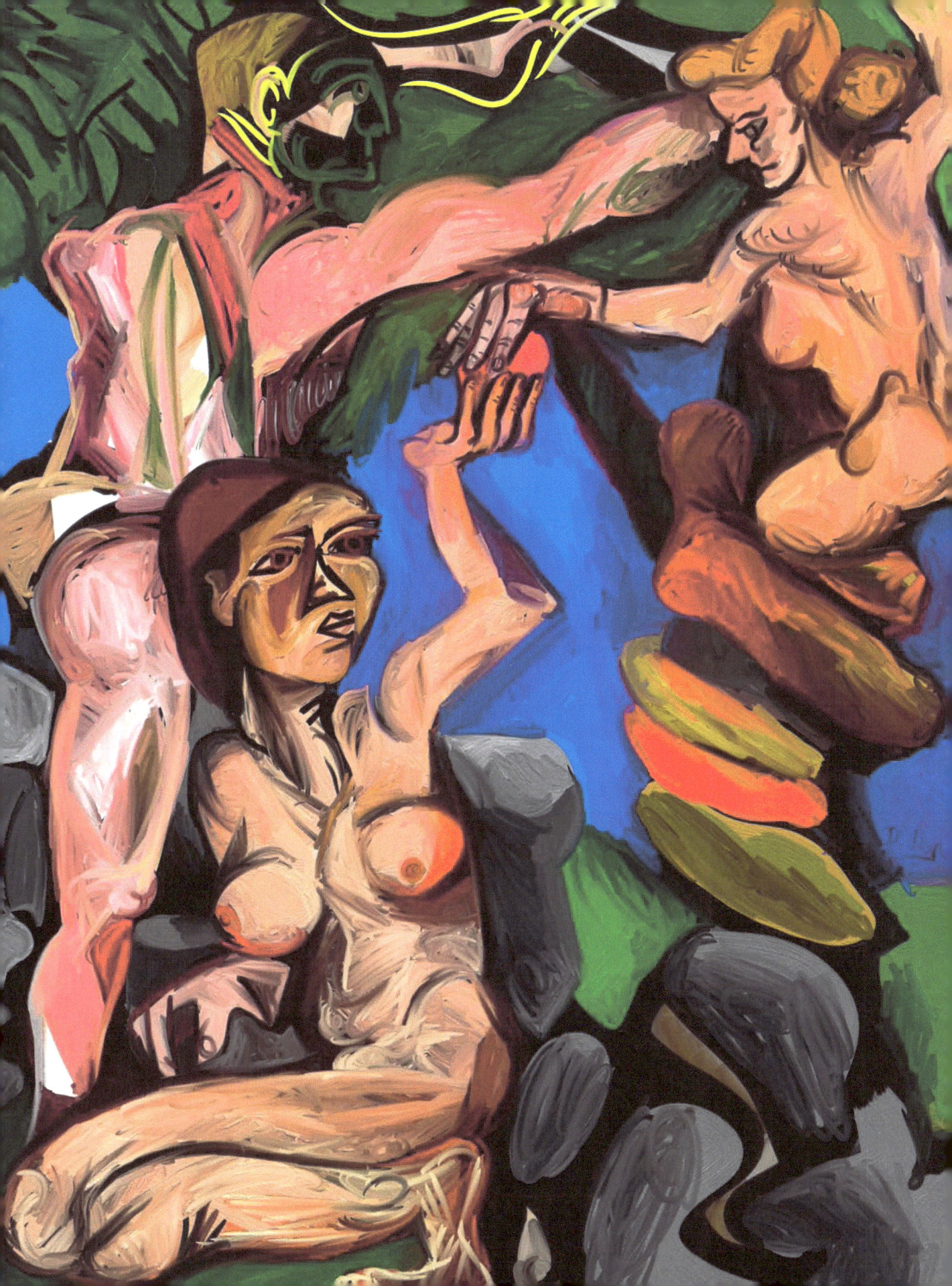

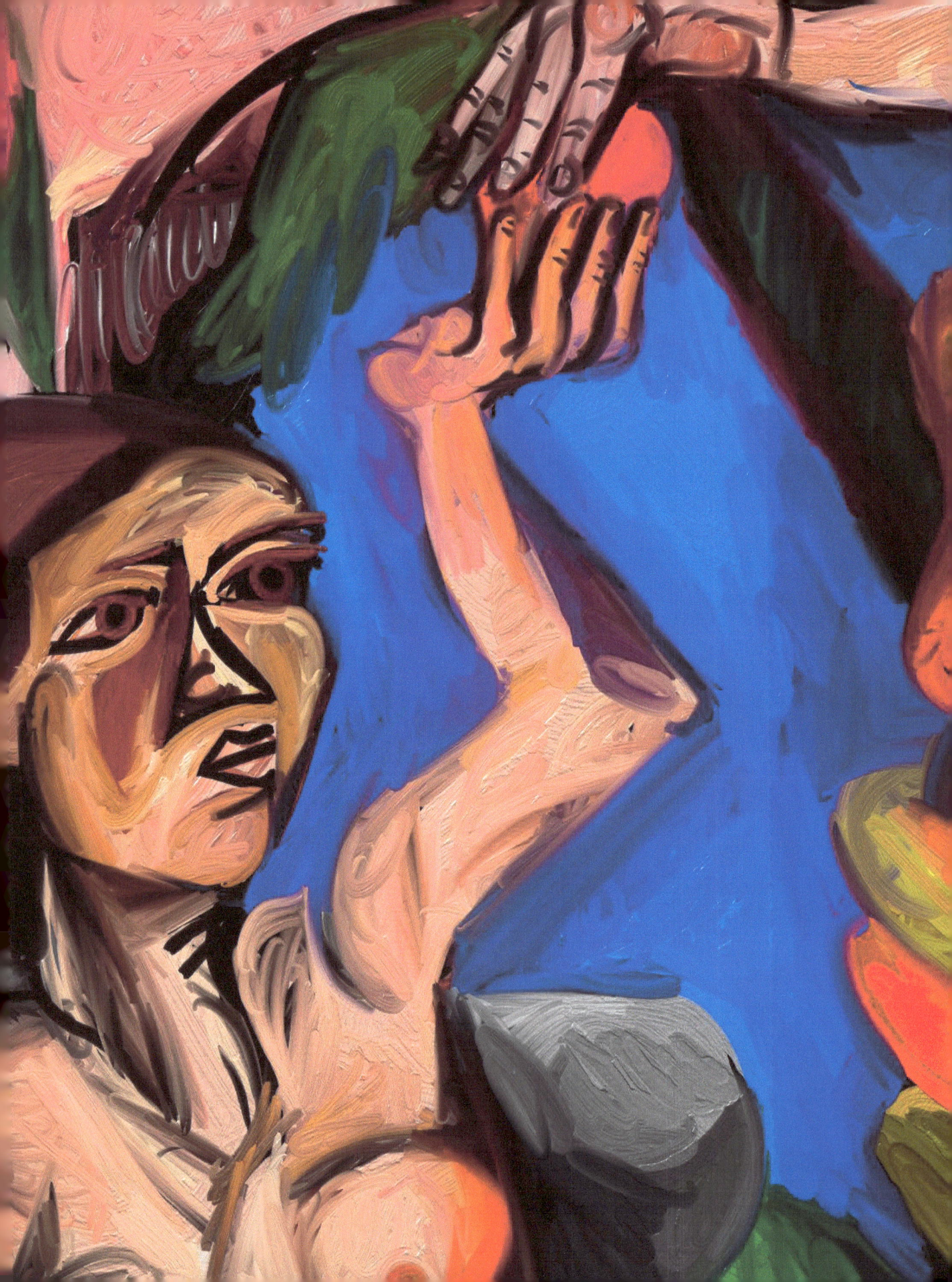

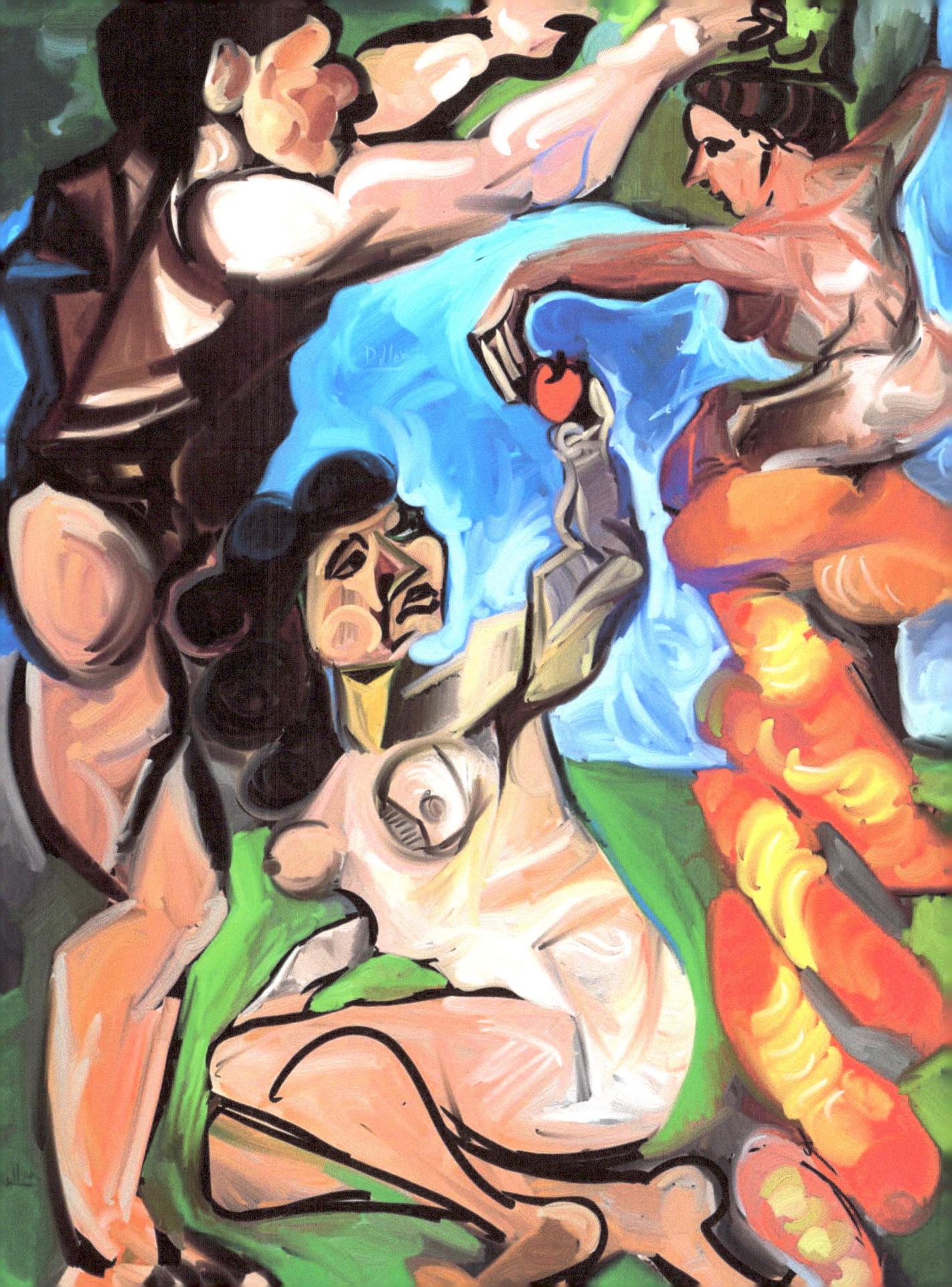

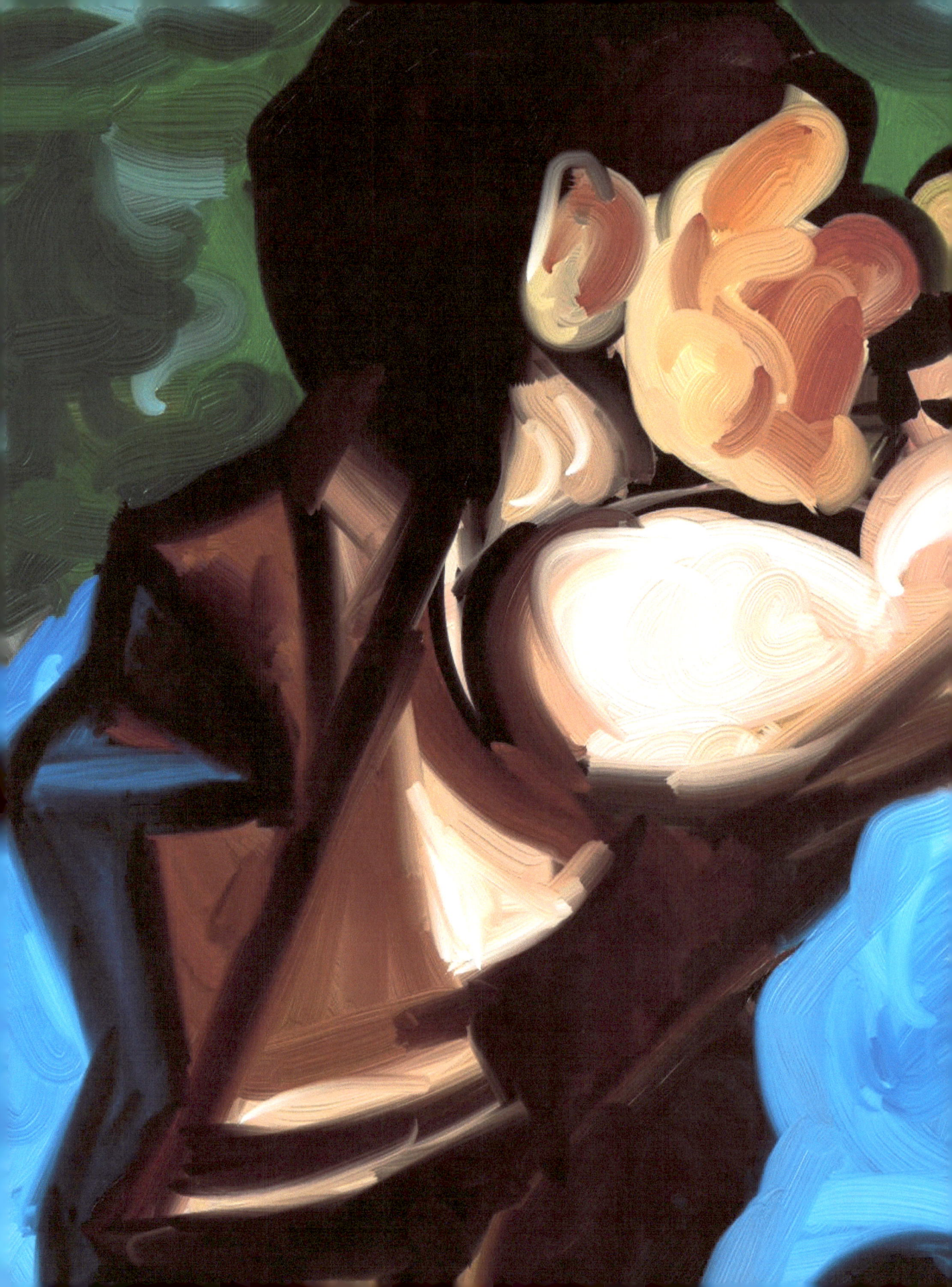

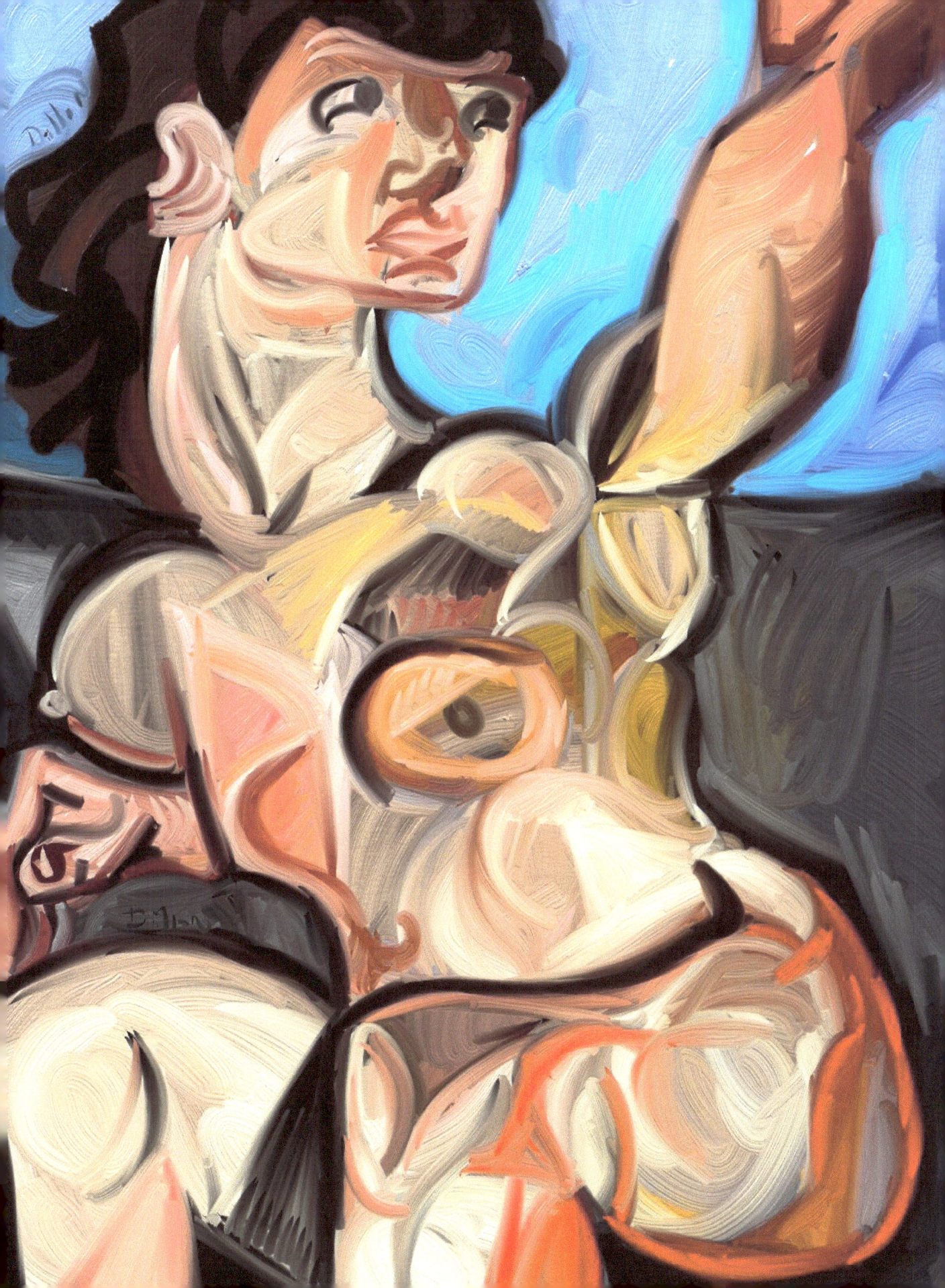

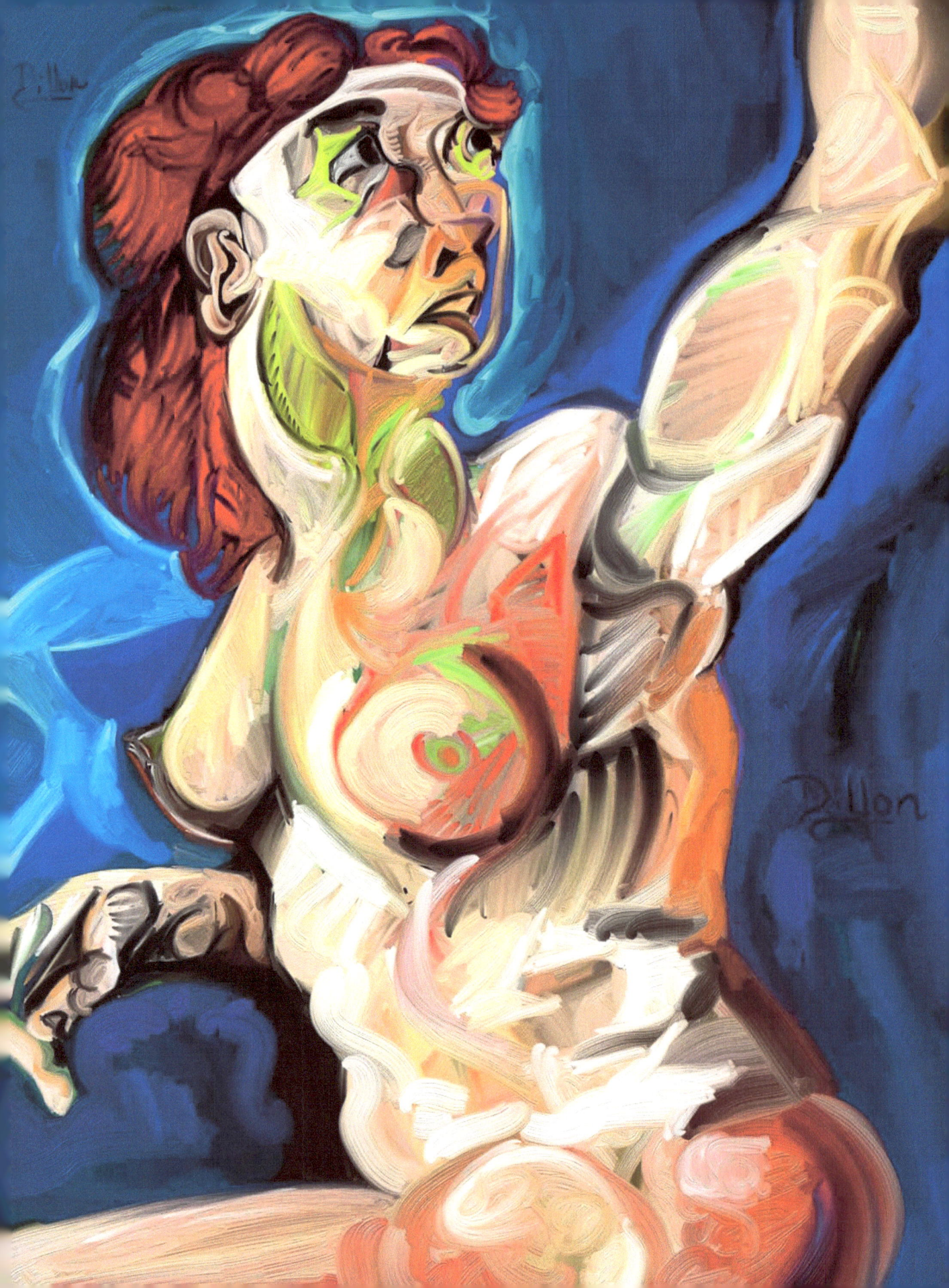

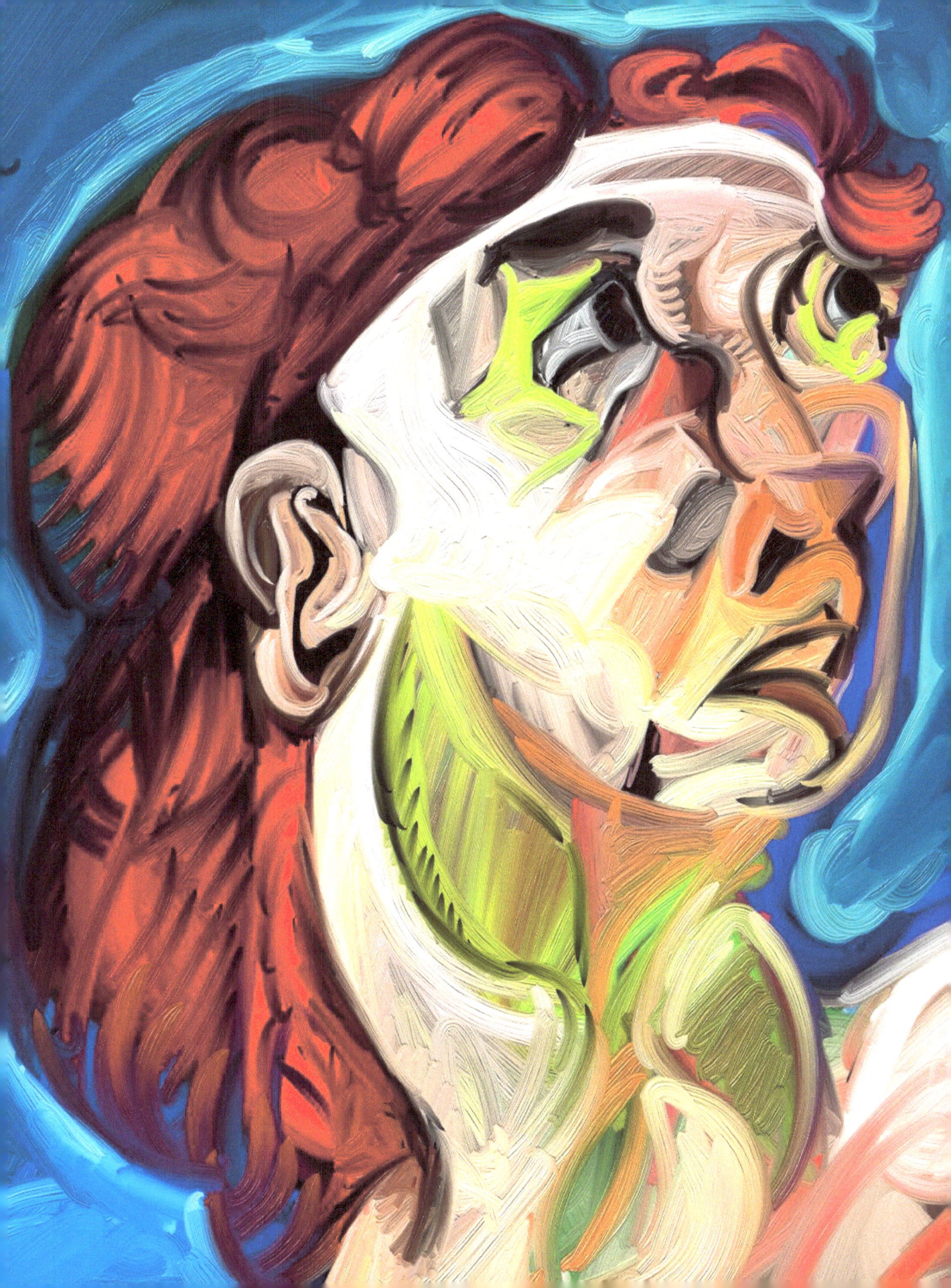

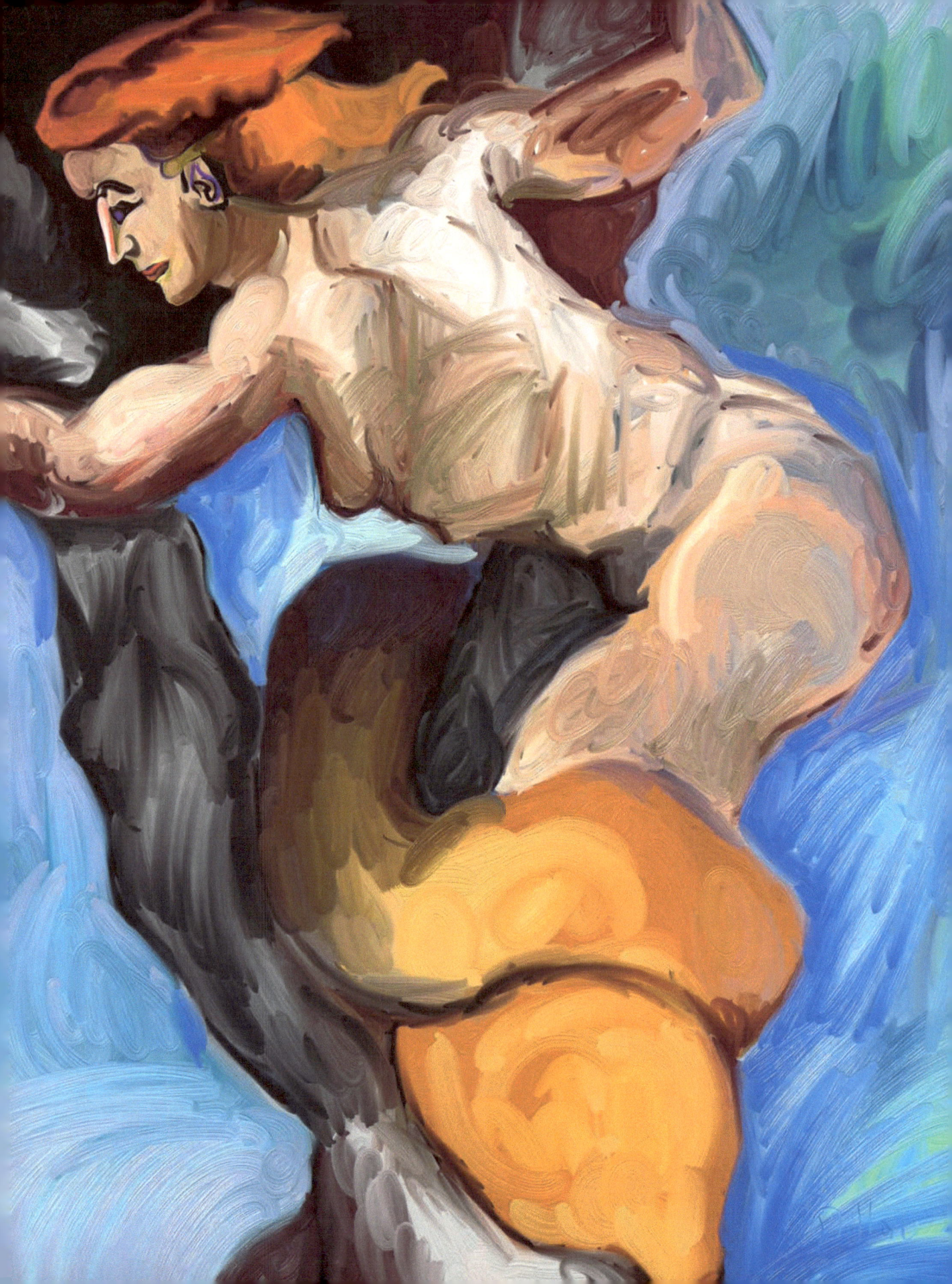

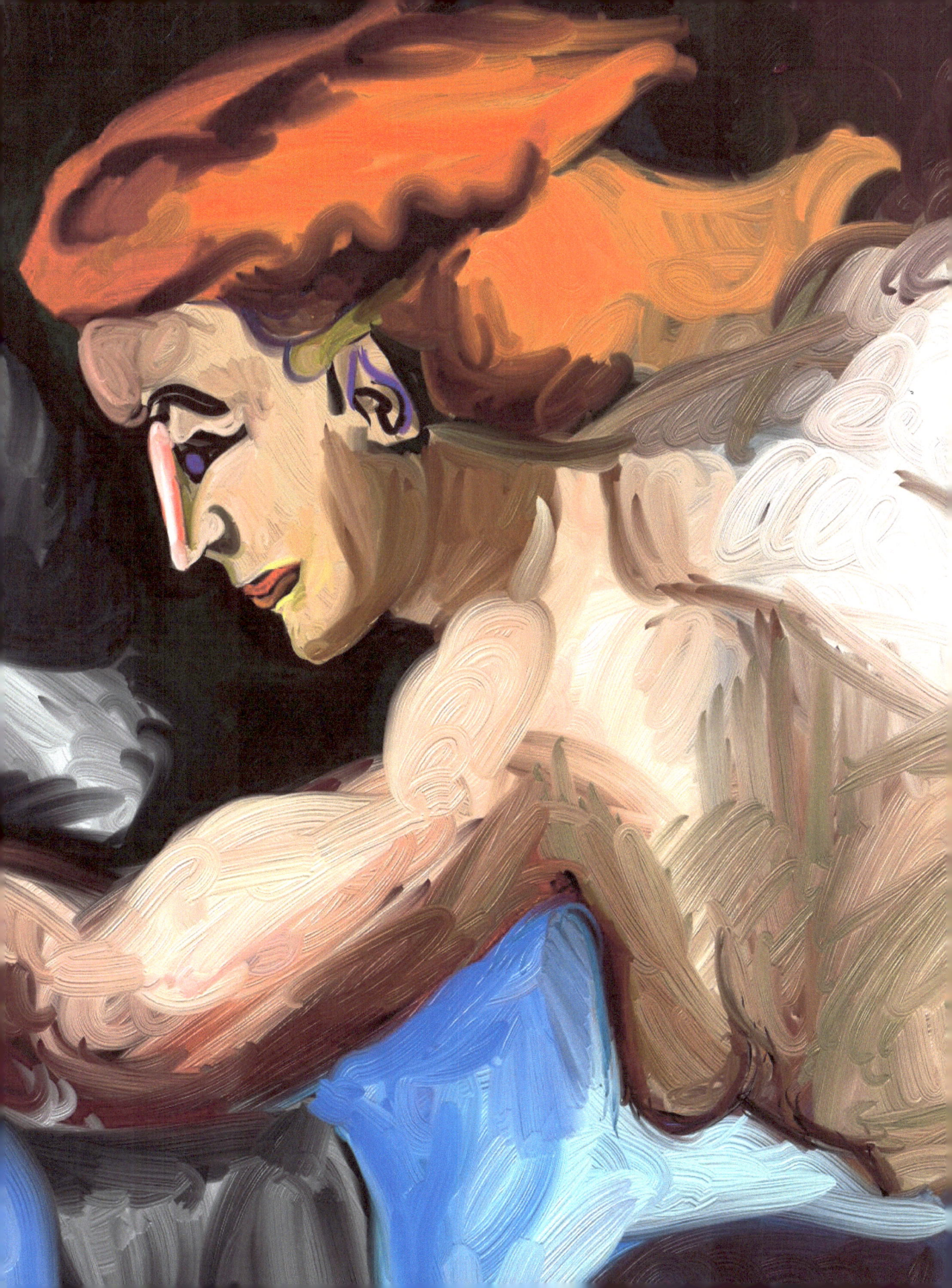

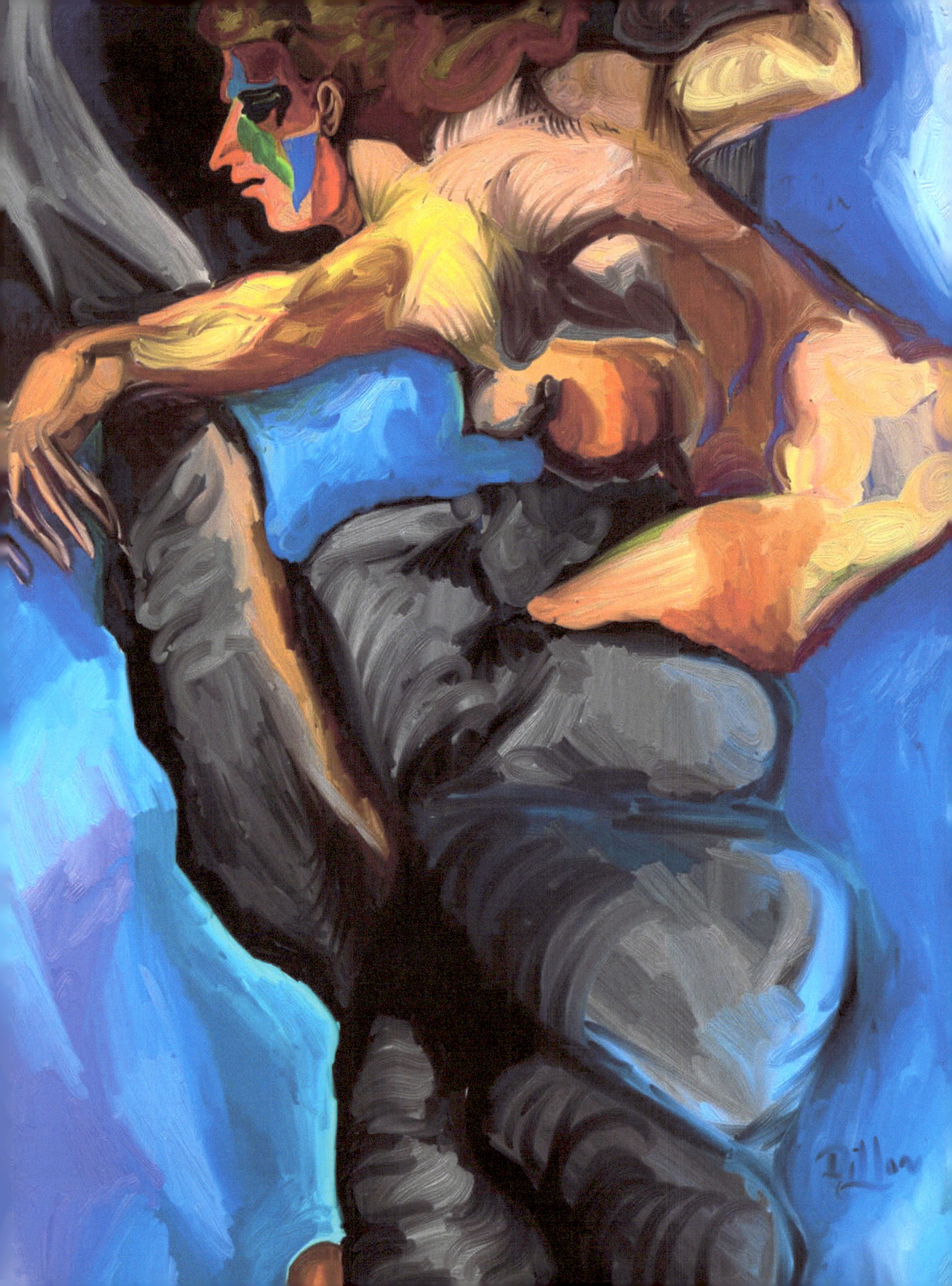

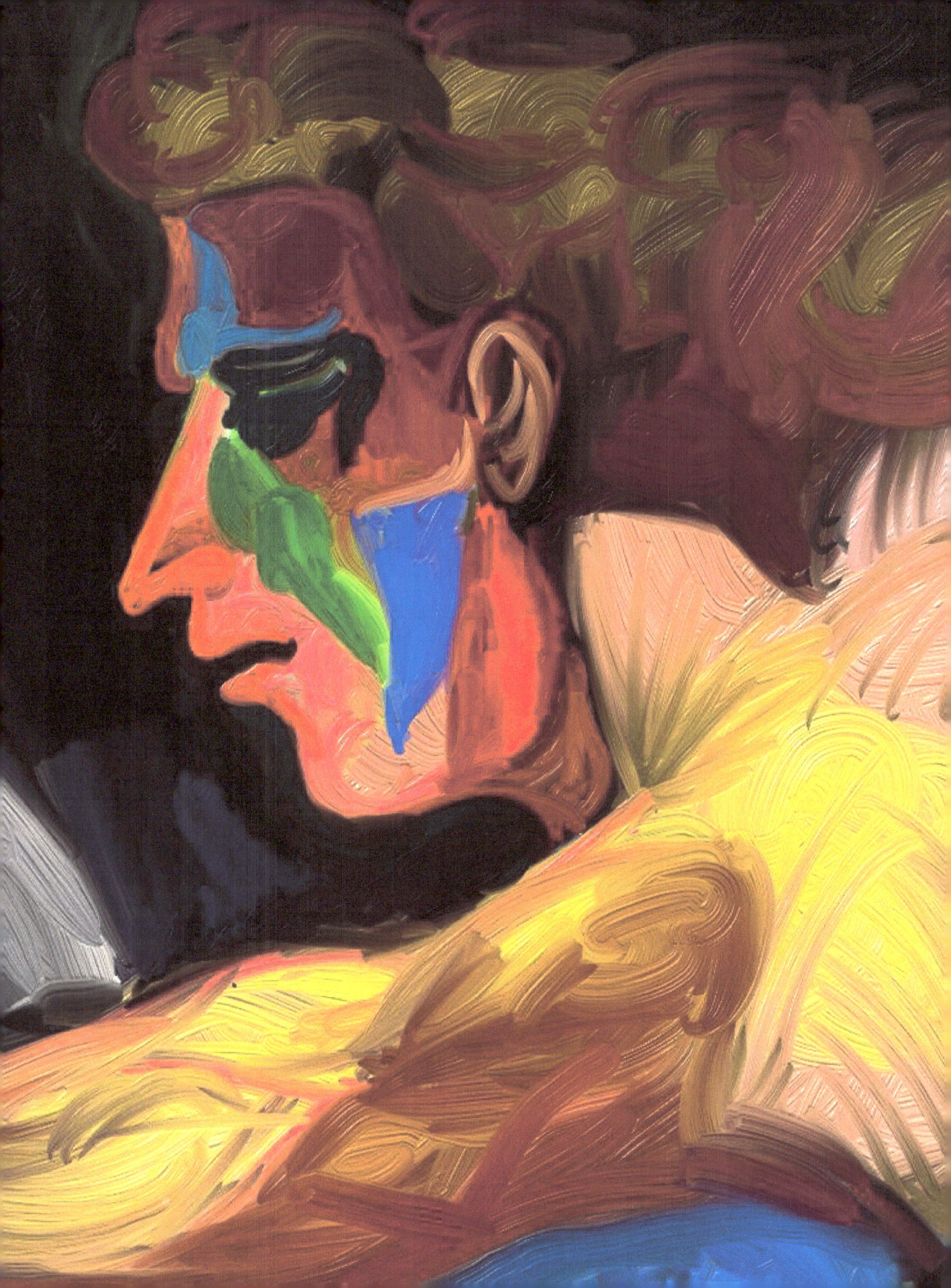

Expulsion

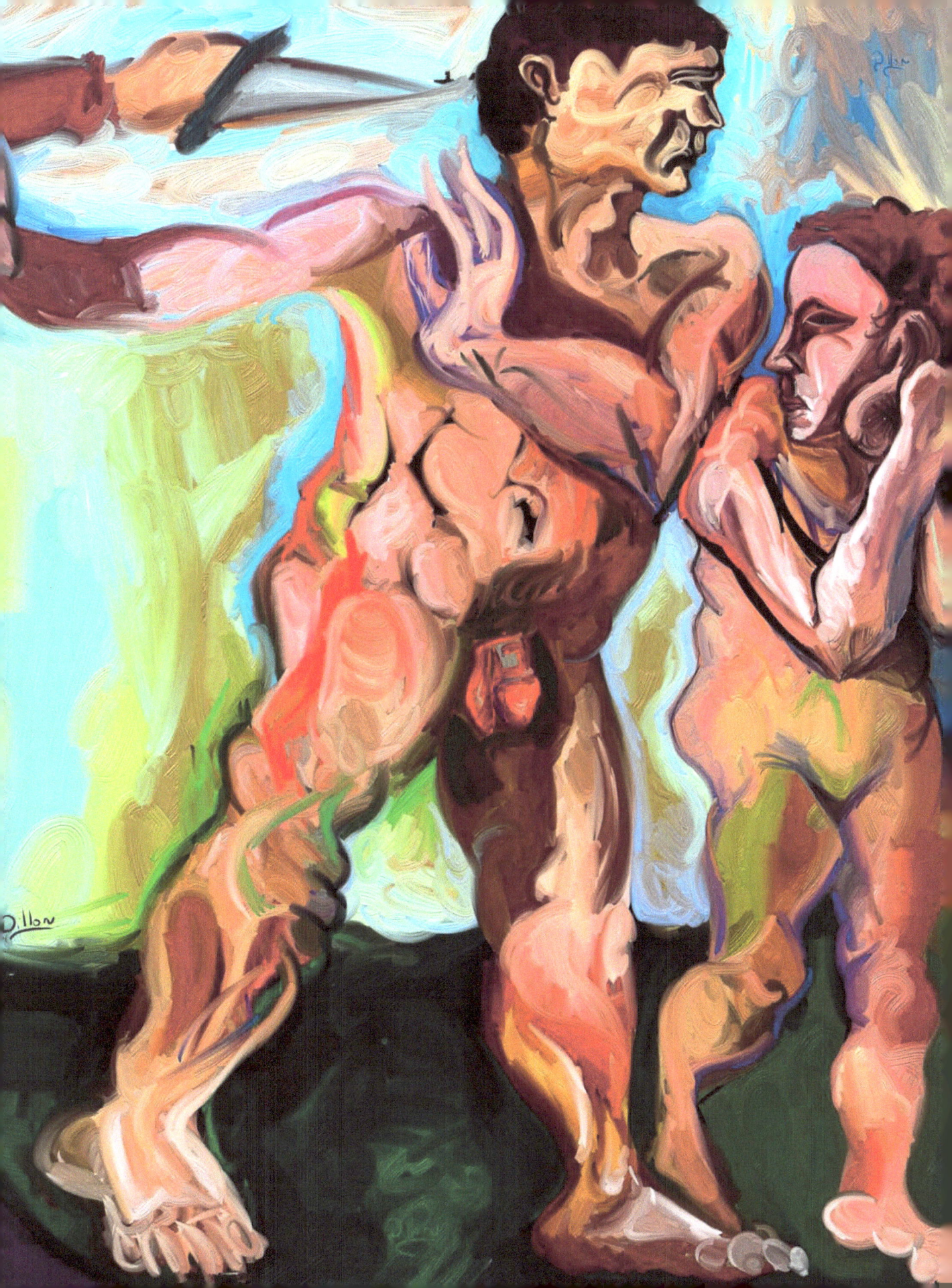

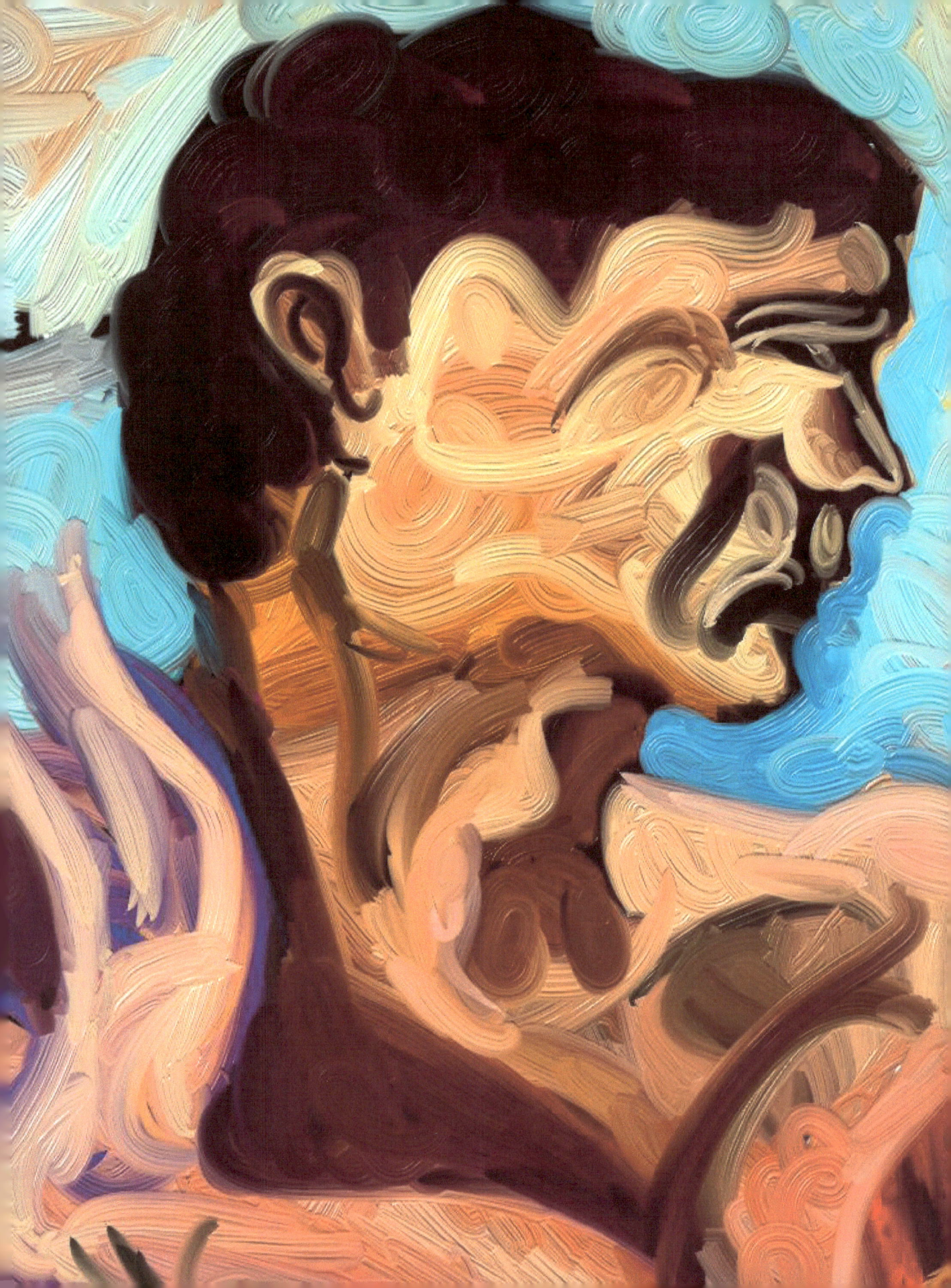

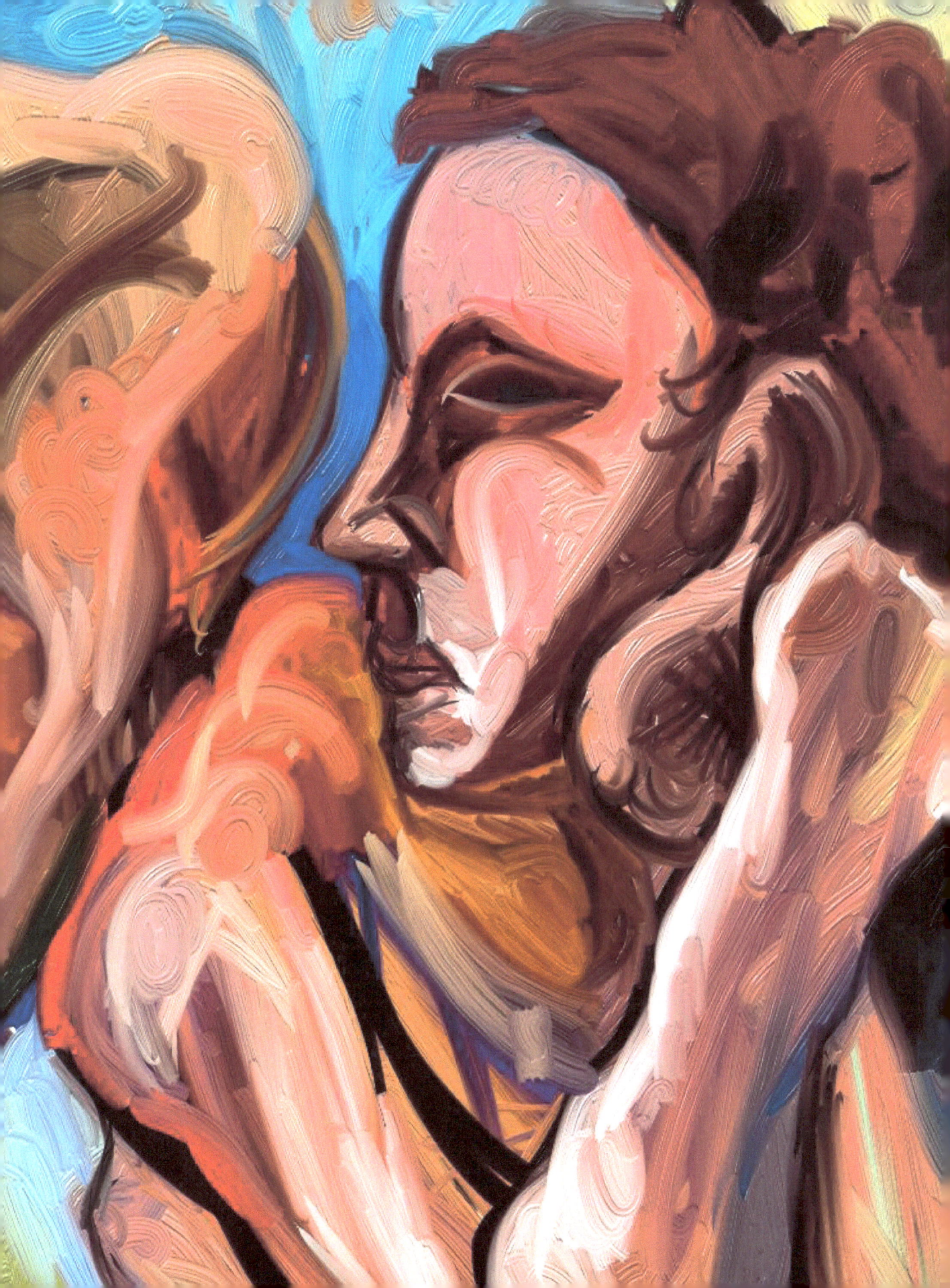

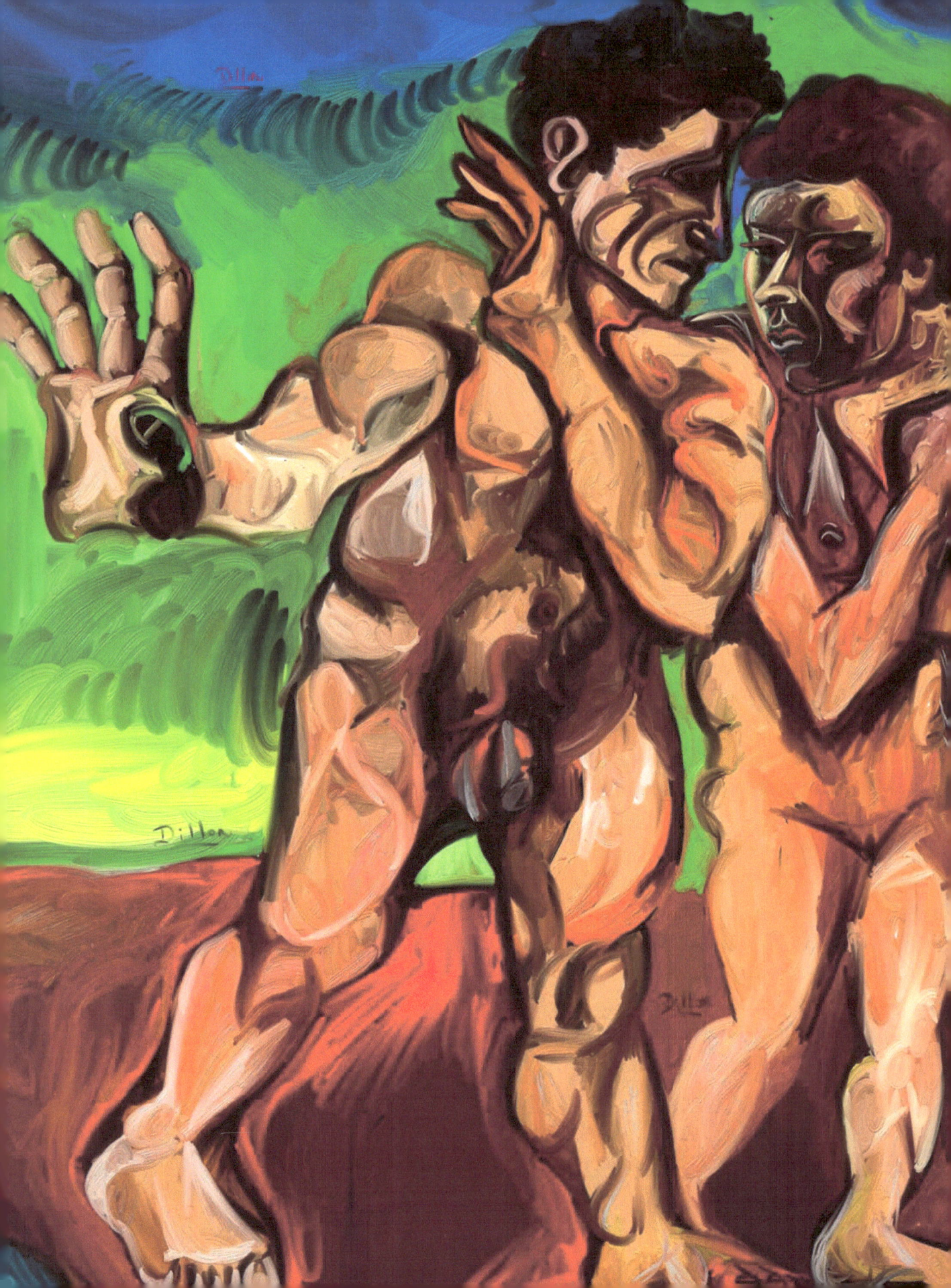

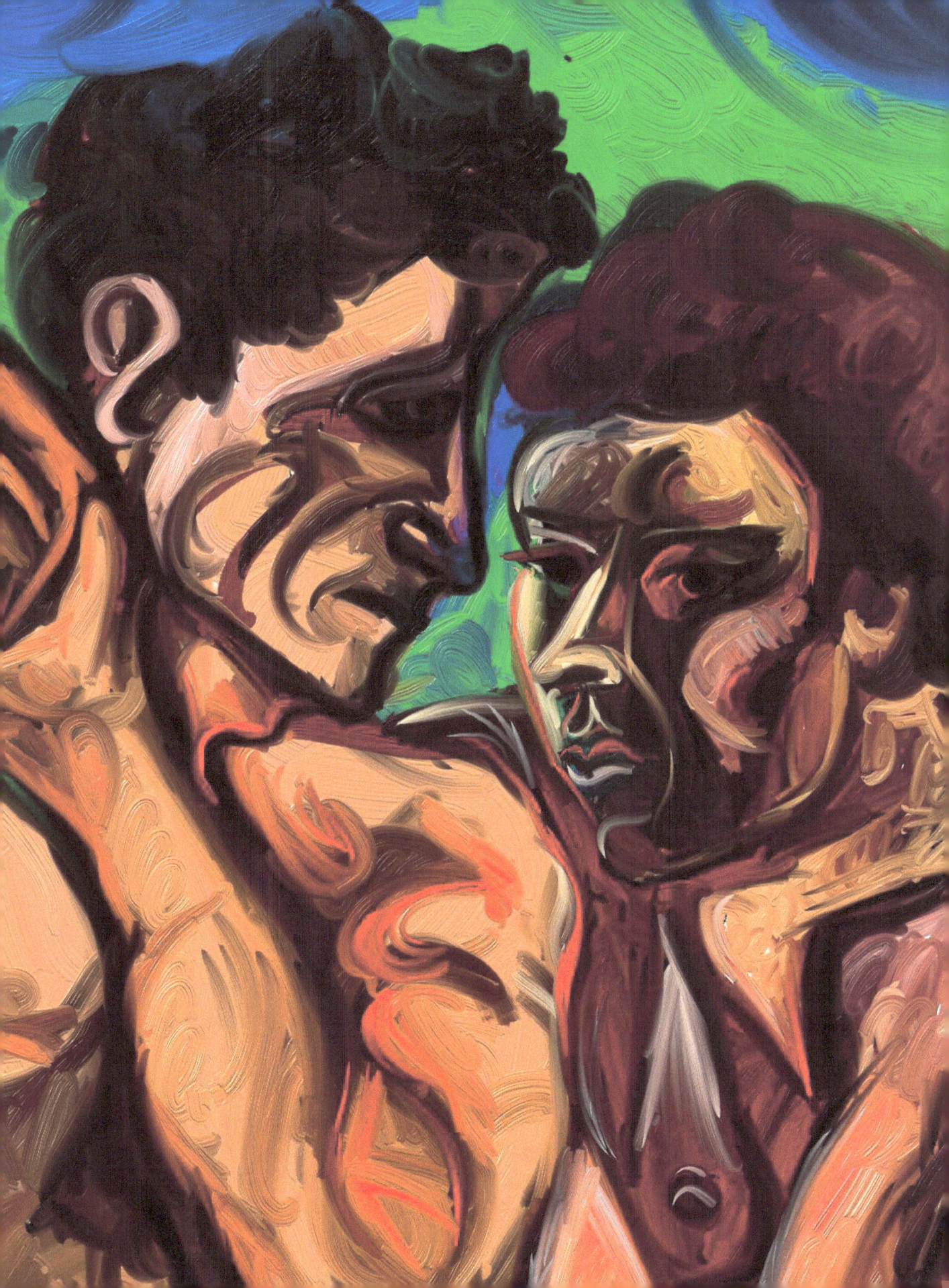

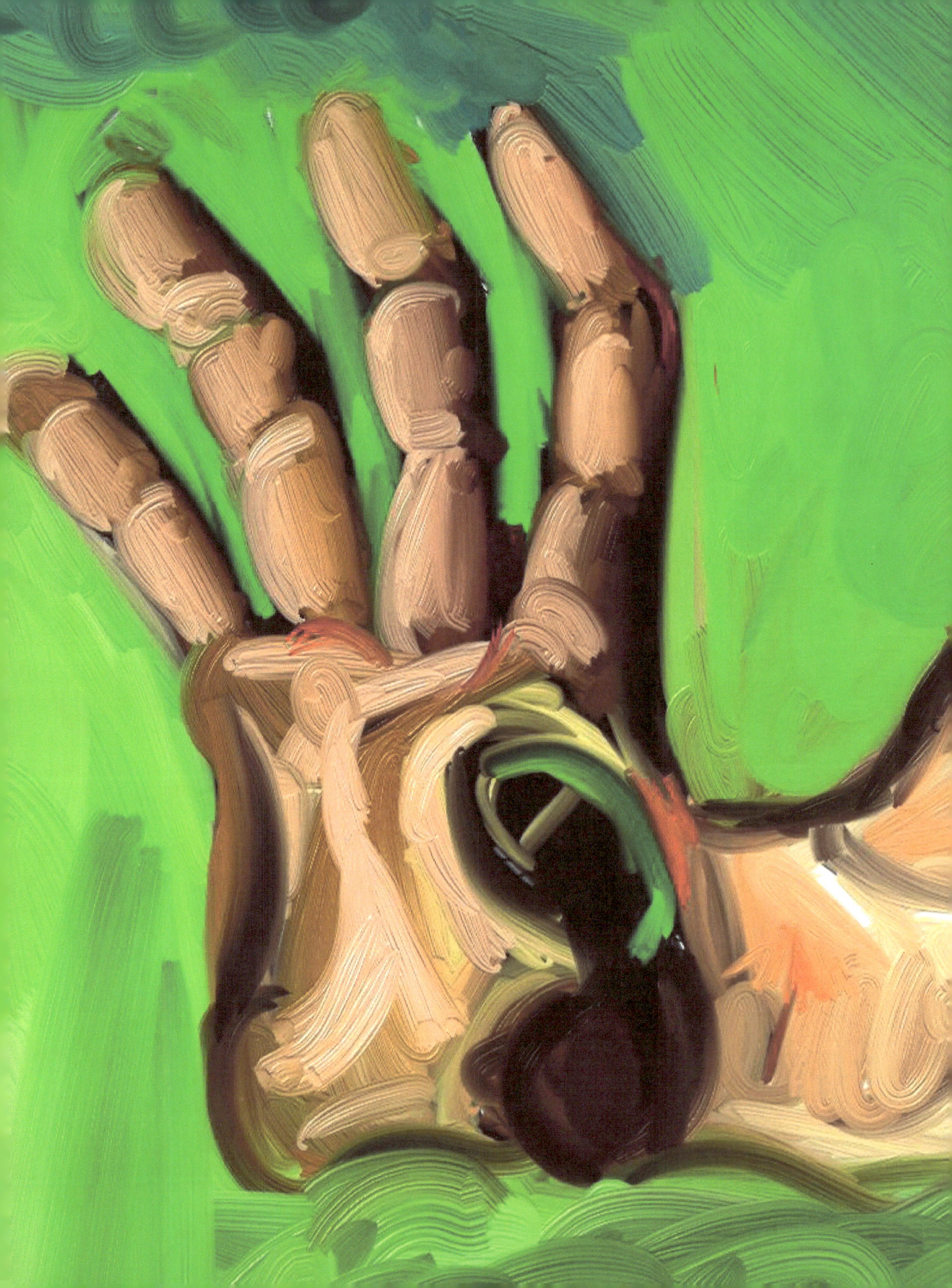

The end.

Other Books from Veroglyphic Publishing

- The Artist and Aesop (Available on Amazon)